This book is dedicated to
Stephanie and Francesco

ISBN: 1-4392-6771-5
ISBN-13: 9781439267714

A HEALTHY DIET
FOR YOUR
Mind AND *Soul*

A True Story That Will Enlighten and
Empower Your Life's Journey

[signature]

Book #2

STEPHEN CITO
MOTIVATIONAL/INSPIRATIONAL SPEAKER

www.mindvisioninspired.com

Contents

Introduction
To my valued readers: Why I wrote this book

My purpose and the intent in writing this book is to share with the reader a truth, clarity, and a positive vision and understanding on our way of being that I have come to know and experience. Let's face it, we have been given life from the start, and we took our first breath, and we have been living life ever since. At birth we had no teachings or knowledge of life. We had no life experience. At birth we grew up in the environments and the surroundings we lived in. The early teachings of our parents and caregivers developed our way of being. We were all precious newborns at the time of our birth. Over our lifetime, our surroundings, teachings, experiences, and responsibilities (or lack of them) made us who we are today.

So here you are. You have become who you are through the experiences of what has been said and done to you and what you have said and done to others. You have been given this power to define who you are. The questions I ask are: Do you know who you truly are? Are you happy with whom you are? Do you have any conflict in your life, or are you at peace with yourself and everyone around you?

I can truly say in the early stages of my life, I was told and experienced certain things that were not true about me. I became a product of my environment. I discovered the real truth about me as I grew into an adult. I believe it takes time, self reflection, responsibility, and life experiences to have an understanding of who you truly are. A good life fulfilled with love, peace, prosperity, and freedom is no accident. There is a certain understanding, and a way of being in life to achieve this.

I have put forty-five years of life experience into this book. I encourage you, as unique and as precious as you are, to open your heart and mind to the words I have written. If you do so, I can truly say that you will live a fulfilled life, as it was intended to be lived from the first day you were born. You will realize that the real truth about you is that you are a wonderful, beautiful human being. My support is with you. God bless you.

Chapter One
The First Breath of Life

With your first breath, you were given life. From that moment forward, you journeyed through life to where you are now and who you have become. In the beginning, you were born a complete, wonderful, beautiful human being. By using your senses naturally in the early stages of life, you developed certain experiences and feelings from your surroundings.

The stage was set before you were born. All the main characters were in place: your mother, father, siblings, if any, followed by secondary characters, including aunts, uncles, cousins, and grandparents. Your parents and relatives had also journeyed a life previously set by their main characters.

Being born into your family, you developed a "way of being" through their teachings and experiences.

They instilled in you their knowledge, customs, beliefs, and life feelings. Through your parents, family, and your surroundings, and by being highly receptive and extremely sensitive in the beginning, you developed what I call a "way of being."

As human beings of love, a natural instinct is the need for love and closeness and to have a sense of connection between our families and our surroundings. The loving intimacy of the parent is a very important part of a newborn's upbringing. We are dependent on our parents and caregivers to provide us with all the necessities of life, including food, shelter, and clothing. Our natural instincts drive us to depend on our parents and caregivers entirely to provide all other necessities of life to us. Our parents play an important role in the development of our way of being in the early stages of life. As children, we depend on our parents as our first teachers and observe everything they do and say. In return, we become a by-product of who they are. Our parents teach us what they know through their life experiences, from what has been done and what has been said to them. For example, if a parent has been in an abusive relationship with his or her parents, in return the result and the pattern may continue with their children.

The pattern of behaviour between parents and their children are inherited. The cycle of behaviour can go back several generations of family history. This cycle will continue until the parent or the adolescent child becomes **"aware"** and chooses to break the cycle and change his or her way of being.

To follow this understanding, one must be open and compassionate, to look back to his or her family history. One must have an understanding of the dynamics within his or her family. Having compassion and understanding are the first crucial steps in moving forward towards a fulfilling life.

The Truth of Who You Are

You are a wonderful, beautiful human being. This is the truth of who you are. You were born that way. You are also able to see the beauty that lies within a young child or even an adult whose inner way of being may be affected physically or mentally. No matter your physical or mental state, the soul is always intact.

You are where you are, who you are because of your life experiences and your beliefs about what has happened in your life and how you have dealt with it. As we journey through our childhood and into our adult life, we become distracted from our core foundation and the truth of who we really are. We allow our surroundings and experiences to define who we believe we are, and we give power to fear and other influences that control our lives. We blame ourselves for the things that have happened to us and take blame for wrongs brought upon us. We inherit and take on pain and responsibility for the actions of others, and we blame ourselves for it.

Through this misguided way of being, we pull further and further from the truth of who we truly are. We become distracted from our true way of being, focusing more on the expectations of others, rather than who we should be. We place more energy and effort into trying to fit in, and we worry more about what other people might think or say about us. The heart and mind become separated and out of sync with one another.

The sense of being becomes more of an illusion than it is reality. You develop a belief system that does not reflect the truth about yourself or even that of others. The greatest example of a way of being is a child between the ages of three and five. The child lives in the moment and doesn't care about yesterday or tomorrow. An adult who has journeyed in life to rediscover the beauty and greatness that lies within eliminates past misconceptions and beliefs to be in the place of that three- to five-year-old child, living life in the present moment, not caring about yesterday. That person can only look forward to tomorrow. When was the last time you jumped in a puddle, had fun doing it, and couldn't be concerned about getting wet? Knowing that you are a wonderful, beautiful human being is the truth and the greatest place to be. A lie can be told in many ways, but there is only one truth. Knowing your core foundation will set you free. By eliminating all the lies, distractions, and misconceptions of our life experiences, we can reclaim our true identity and take ourselves back to the wonderful human being we've always been.

Heart and Mind

The mind is very powerful. You must take control of your mind or your mind will take control of you. Everything starts with a thought. When you look around and see and experience what the mind has created, the imagination is endless. The infinite mind can create endless possibilities. A thought is the starting point of something. When you place movement or action to your thought, it will manifest and become something. A thought without action or movement is just a thought. A dream works the same way. Having a dream is simply a dream until you take action and make it real. Heart and mind work together. The heart feels pain through mind experiences. It filters signals received from the mind. The results are a happy and pleasant heart, or a sad and unhappy one. Through mind experiences, the heart may experience light or darkness, or it may experience high or low energy. Your mind experiences (or thoughts) control your moods, they also control the way you choose to live. You choose your life on how you think (mind) and how you feel (heart).

You may have been asked at some point, "What are your thoughts"? Or "What do you think"? You must be able to feel out a situation not only have thoughts about it. This is a way of centering yourself so your mind (thoughts) and your heart are connected and in sync with one another. When your mind is inspired and in line with your heart, with a positive way of thinking the heart and mind work together. This is a powerful mindset to have. A positive vision with inspiration, followed by positive action, is a united force to a higher awareness of your greater potential, power, purpose, and possibilities. The greatest results are achieved when you mix positive thinking with inspiration.

Over the years, through the existence of humanity, we have witnessed time after time, the incredible results achieved when one mixes positive inspiration with his or her way of thinking. The same understanding applies when someone is driven and inspired with a negative way of thinking. One can achieve results through negative inspiration, but the results can be devastating. As the old saying goes, "Goodness comes from the heart." When you put your heart into your thoughts, and you are inspired to do something, the results usually work in your favour. For example, if you watch a sporting event, and the team has won a championship, some of the players will say things like, "We put our hearts and souls into winning;" "We gave it all we had," or "I felt driven and inspired to win." When you place your energy, whether in a positive way or a negative way of thinking, it will in return create a result. It is important to always manage your way of thinking, and think first before you do or say anything. A true leader will always think first before he or she reacts. If you move too far ahead of yourself you miss out on what has passed, and you make assumptions and speculations that can lead to lack of clarity and confusion. You must take two steps back to clearly see two steps forward.

The Thoughts and Energy that Surround Us

Our mind processes thousands of thoughts each day. Our way of thinking is our way of being. The way we think is what appears. Our thoughts and emotions also work together to create a result. Since our thoughts create energy, we live our lives by how we think. How you are thinking is how you are being. If you have a thought that upsets you and your emotions tie into that thought, you may become angry, which is an emotion connected with your thought. If you have a thought that inspires you and makes you feel good, you may have a smile on your face and feel at ease, which is an emotion connected to your thought. If we become subconsciously aware of something, it appears.

I once purchased a silver vehicle. I drove this vehicle for three years. When the lease was up, I decided to purchase the same vehicle. When the car salesman called me to inform me that he had one in stock, I was interested. He said that the color was white and that, if I was interested, he suggested I take a look at it. I had no clue what this vehicle looked like, because I was used to seeing one in silver. I tried to imagine what it looked like, but I couldn't visualize it in my mind. So I made an appointment with the car salesman to see the vehicle. Not knowing what to expect, the contrast of white with black trim was pleasing to the eye so I purchased the vehicle. From that day forward I became aware of the white vehicle. You see, the vehicle and the color was always there, I just wasn't aware of it. What you are aware of is what will appear. This applies to everything in life. Being in tune with yourself and your surroundings makes you aware of what is and what appears.

Positive and Negative Thinking

The mind is constantly working. It thinks 24/7. There isn't a time when the mind is not working. Even when we are asleep, the mind is thinking. The mind will either create a way of positive thinking or negative thinking. Associated with this way of thinking is the energy that is combined with our way of thinking.

If you focus on the words *positive* and *negative* in relation to mathematics, you will see that positive (+) will add more and negative (-) will subtract or take away. In relation to thinking, one who creates positive thoughts will progress forward, achieve more in life, and have more energy. One who creates negative thoughts will set him or her back, take away all that's before him or her in life, and have less energy or momentum. We are in combat with positive and negative thoughts and the energy that lies within and surrounds us at all times. I relate to this way of thinking as two forces fighting against each other.

Another example is in electricity. You need to separate the positive and negative wires, because if you connect them together, you will get a spark. You must also separate negative and positive thoughts. The more you condition your mind to think positively, the less power negative thoughts have. The more you condition your mind to think negatively, the less power positive thoughts have. Since our way of thinking creates a form of energy, we have the choice each day to decide whether to be more positive and attract positive energy, or we can choose to be more negative, achieve less, attract negative energy, and set ourselves back in life.

Positive thinkers are optimistic and look forward to what the future has in store, leaving their past behind, not dwelling on the negative side of it. Negative thinkers remain stuck in their past by allowing their past experiences to control their present way of being and allow it to be their future. It takes less courage to think in a negative way than to be positive and think positively. You can experience this by listening to people having a conversation. If you listen closely to the conversations around you, it will take you no time to tune into negative suggestions and expressions.

Negative energy is contagious and wasteful. Before you know it, you are caught up in it and are a part of it. We are drawn into negative energy. You don't have to go too far to find it. Negativity lies everywhere you look, in conversations that you hear and in the news. If you want to hear good news, you have to go to it. It takes a will and courage to be a positive thinker and doer. Since negativity comes to us in many ways, we need courage to steer away from it, for it can be influential. One needs to be disciplined in his or her way of thinking and way of being. At the beginning of each day, we have a choice to place our thoughts and energy on either being positive or being negative. The end result of positive thinking is that you win—of negative thinking that you lose!

Thoughts and Expressions

*Thoughts are an illusion and untruthful,
unless they are connected to the heart.*

*Your health is in your hands. For what you place in your
mouth has a great influence on your health.*

Endless Sky:

*Endless sky with no end in sight, connect me to everything
that you see from above. At night when you're asleep, guide
me from above with your shimmering light and bring bright-
ness and closeness to me, so I am able to be in your light.*

A prayer for the unborn child:

*God bless the child within and give it courage and
strength so it will follow the right path in life.*

In the eye of God, we are all born equal. One thing that separates us is ignorance.

Physical beauty disappears over time; the beauty that lies within is everlasting.

A thought is the starting point to something.

The mind is more powerful than the physical, for it takes the mind to move the physical.

Tears are liquid expressions of your life and life feelings that come straight from the heart.

You cannot run away from your own mind or shadow, so think positive and be good to yourself.

*Parents are our first teachers; they have a
great influence in our lives.*

*A lie can be told in many ways, but there's only one truth.
The truth will stand the test of time.*

*You pass on in life what you know and
what you have experienced.*

*The greatest disability one can ever have is the disability of
distorted thinking.*

*I think our greatest teachers in life are children from
the ages of two through five and the adults who have traveled
a journey in life to return back to their inner child.*

Your facial expressions are your inner thoughts and feelings.

Parents, invest all your love in your children.

You attract what you think.

Your visualization with action is your realization.

You are a wonderful, beautiful human being.
It is a simple truth of who you are.

Our children today are the people and families of tomorrow.

What you're being for a living is more important than
what you are doing for a living. What and
how are you being for a living?

NOTES FOR CHAPTER 1

Chapter Two
A True Story

My name is Stephen Cito. I was born into a family of five children. I am also a twin. My parents had five children in less than five years. They are of European descent (Italian). They came to Canada from Southern Italy in the late 1950s to start a new life in a country and a language unknown to them. With high hopes and optimism, they ventured out and created a new chapter in their lives.

Not knowing the hardships that would follow, they had a hard time adjusting to the circumstances in which they found themselves. They had no knowledge of the English language and virtually no money, and they started from the bottom. They soon realized that the new life they wanted would not be easy to achieve. They took nothing for granted and worked hard just to survive, at times working two jobs just to make ends meet.

Within their first five years in Canada, they had five children. If that isn't pressure, I don't know what is. I still wonder to this day why they didn't take their time before raising a family. I guess in those days, aside from work, there wasn't much else for them to do. Through the pressure, hardships, and responsibilities my parents faced, our bringing up as children was not easy. We felt their pressure and hardships in how we were treated.

As a young child, I experienced a tough and disciplined life. There was never any conversation in response to life issues and circumstances. My parents were not given the tools of effective communication by their parents; they never learned to be more self expressive, articulate, and understanding towards their children. They imposed strict rules, and if those rules were not met, discipline would follow, sometimes in the form of physical or emotional abuse. My father would play the lead role of the family as the one in control, and my mother followed the man of the house, so to speak, the one in charge. I was taught at an early age to stand up and fight for myself. "An eye for an eye," as it is called. I had to be strong physically so no one would walk all over me. There would be no conversation when it came to conflict, only the use of physical force.

With the physical and emotional abuse, combined with the lack of closeness and love that I experienced, a character developed within me. This character had low self-esteem, was angry, resentful, and had a lack of appreciation towards him and others that manifested into what we call a bully. When it came to bullying, I was first in my class. No one dared to walk all over me. I watched wrestling on Sundays to keep up with my technical skills, so I was always ready for combat.

In first grade, I was described by my teacher as being distracted and having difficulty learning. Failing in grade one reconfirmed the belief my parents instilled in me that I was not capable or smart enough to succeed. My twin sister moved on to grade two. At age of six, my self-esteem and self-worth diminished.

By the age of twelve, my aggressive behaviour resulted in trouble with the school and the law. I came to realize that something terrible was going on. This had a great impact on my life, and I had to decide at that point which path I was going to choose. If I continued a path of self-destruction and aggressive behaviour, I would only get myself in greater trouble. So I chose to achieve, not destroy. This was a turning point in my life—like an awakening! Through compassion and understanding, I was able to put all the missing pieces in my life together.

I started to place myself in other people's shoes and was able to understand, through compassion, what was happening in my life. At the age of fourteen, I realized how difficult it was to earn a pay check. Working with my uncle in construction taught me a valuable lesson in life: you have to work to earn a living. This experience helped me realize how hard it had been for my parents to make a living, so I came to admire their role, responsibilities, hard work, and determination to create a comfortable life for the family. Through high school, I was recognized for my talent and respected by the music program, and I built close relationships with fellow students and teachers. At this point, I built up my self-esteem and realized that through hard work and determination, I could achieve anything I wanted in life. This was a very important life experience for me.

When I completed high school, I decided to be a hairstylist. This was not great news for my father; his father had been a barber in Europe and made little money. I got no support from my parents regarding my career, so I had to depend on myself. I worked a full summer and part-time to save for my tuition. My parents felt that I should've been a doctor or a lawyer and to have an education that they were not able to have. I envisioned through my career the success that I would achieve through hard work and determination as I experienced in high school. I succeeded by being passionate and driven.

One day, my father was sitting in my styling chair, and we had a conversation as I was cutting his hair.

"Dad, remember when you used to tell me that your grandfather didn't succeed as a barber and chances were that I was not going to succeed as a hairstylist?"

"Yes."

"Well, if you look at what I've achieved over the years, I would think that I've done okay for myself and succeeded.

He replied, "You have succeeded. I just never thought you had it in you to succeed."

I had to clear this up with him. I replied, "You were not able to see it through yourself to succeed; therefore, you were not able to see it in me to succeed."

He paused, and response, "You're right."

If an individual is not able to see it in themselves to achieve or succeed, how can they possibly see it in someone else? I continued my journey in life, came to understand my role and the role of my parents. Through compassion, understanding, forgiveness, and love—these four ingredients—I was able to reclaim a wonderful relationship with my parents and let go of the pain of past issues in my relationship with them. I realized the true love, respect, and admiration my parents had for me. I also realized that the experience my father had with his father was similar to the relationship he had with me. We are who we are from what we know and what we have experienced. We only do differently when we change our way of thinking and way of being.

As I continued on in life, I focused on being productive and responsible towards my family. I was blessed in having two wonderful kids. My parents taught me a very valuable lesson in parenting; they taught me what not to do to my children. All I had to do was simply the opposite of what my parents did to me in raising my children. I chose to break the cycle, take responsibility for my actions, and follow a different path as a parent. There was no physical or emotional abuse towards my children. I instilled positive thoughts and encouragement in them, so they were able to be who they were meant to be—wonderful, beautiful human beings. I would tuck my kids into bed at night, and they would tell me bedtime stories that I was never told as a child. Parents are the greatest influence and teachers of their children. The child has a connection with the parents at birth and learns from their teachings first. I cannot stress enough to the parents the importance of this understanding.

As the years progressed, I felt that something wasn't right. I went to personal counselling to search for answers and clarity about my personal life. As I took responsibility searching for answers combined with courage and determination, I continued on the path of self discovery and realized that I was all alone. I was tired of living still. On Monday, December 4, 2006, I was home alone with no answers in sight. I searched the Internet for answers. Without any solutions and answers

I felt trapped. I couldn't move forward, sideways, or up and down, and I was exhausted from trying to find a solution. At 3:30 in the afternoon, I made a choice and decided to turn towards myself, within, and eliminate something I didn't want any more. I had to eliminate the distorted thoughts and beliefs that were flowing through me from my past and let it go. So I then wrote everything on paper that was flowing through me that didn't feel right. Whatever thought, expression, or word surfaced that didn't feel right I wrote down. It was extremely emotional, for it all surfaced. I then needed to get rid of the paper I had written on. I thought if I simply threw the paper away in the garbage, it would still be there. If I flushed it down the toilet in pieces it would still remain in the pipes. So I decided to burn it. I took the crumbled paper outside, put it in a steel pale and burnt it. As the paper was burning, I said these exact words to myself:

The bad spirit has passed. It no longer exists in me, for it is in the burning depth of evil and no longer here. I, this day, will embrace in the beginning, a pure wholesome spirit, full of love, compassion, peace, and understanding. There is no other than the good, for the tender loving voice has said so.

After completing what I said to myself, the paper burnt completely and I could see white smoke moving upwards from the steel pail. There wasn't a bit of white paper left to burn. I then released the ashes and went inside and wrote on paper those exact words. I felt a sense of relief and realized later on that this was the starting point to the passage of my freedom. For the first time, I forgave myself for any wrongdoing and any pain that I had inflicted on myself and anyone else. You see, it is possible to forgive someone who has hurt you or done something wrong to you, but the hardest person to forgive is yourself. We take so much ownership of what happens to us in our life. We tend to believe it, especially when others point the finger at us saying it's our fault. We blame ourselves and take responsibility for other people's pain. My point and truth is this: *It was never yours to start off with! It was given to you by someone else! So don't take what isn't yours! LET it go!*

When we cannot deal with the pain and issues in our lives, what is one of the first things we do? We pass it on to someone else, blame them for it, and make them the cause. We pass it on from person to person, relationship to relationship, family to family, until someone breaks the pattern. I believe to have peace and freedom in your life, you must be able to forgive everyone who has done any wrong to you or hurt you in any way. You must be able to also forgive yourself. You may say, "I can't forgive and let go of what so and so has done to me; it wasn't fair; they had no right to treat me that way; it's just too painful." By forgiving anyone and everyone who has done any wrong to you and by also forgiving yourself, you *release yourself* from any wrongdoing or pain that has entered your life. By letting go, you are doing it for *yourself*, not anyone else, reclaiming your power and the truth of which you truly are—a wonderful, beautiful human being. I believe if you hold onto past life experiences of hurt, pain, guilt, and so forth, you hold back on life. It's like serving time in prison. You are serving time or feeling imprisoned or trapped because you have a hard time letting go. So you need to ask yourself, "Do I want to continue serving time and feeling trapped, taking responsibility for the issues and the pain that I have, feeling hopeless, powerless, and imprisoned, or do I let it go?" Until you truly let go and forgive, you will always be a part of the pain and issues that were given to you. You need to separate yourself from all of it. Only then will you be able to move on and have a life full of freedom, peace, and harmony.

Two days after burning the paper, everything was quite normal, except for the early afternoon of December 6. At about 2:30 in the afternoon, the sky had darkened. Everything was dark, and it seemed like night. It was unusual for that time of day. That night I went to bed as usual. The following morning, my alarm clock woke me at seven o'clock. As I became conscious and fully awake, my bedroom was full of bright sunlight. The light was really intense and bright. I started to feel something that I had never felt before. All I could think about was reaching out to people of my past and my present to tell them how wonderful and beautiful they were. I made a list of the people I wanted to contact and apologize to. From that moment on, I could not hate anyone. The experience was like waking up to the feelings and voice of my heart. It felt like someone had taken a hose and washed away every distorted thought and negative feelings within me. I felt totally cleansed, pure, and wholesome, and I felt at peace. Just like the way I was when I was first born—wholesome and good. The feelings were unbelievable. I couldn't believe what was going on. I didn't know what to make of it. I felt free. As these feelings were flowing through me that day, I wrote these exact words:

December 7, 2006

I have awakened to the voice of my heart (inner spirit). All good thoughts, intentions, and feelings are surfacing. It has been exactly three days (December 4) since I was able to forgive and let go of my distorted and misled soul within me. It seems uncontrollable. Beautiful expressions, thoughts, words, and ideas are flourishing. I have journeyed forty-five years to come to this day. The feelings are unbelievable for the bad spirit has passed on. Thank you, God.

On the morning of December 8, 2006, when I awoke, these words came to me:

Angel, descend upon me with your guiding light and grant me peace and love, for I am the divine.

After writing those words, I realized for the first time in my life my true identity. If you look at the words closely, you will see what I mean; Angel, descend upon me (send me your message) with your guiding Light (allow me to see in light) and grant me peace and love (being at peace and feeling loved within) for I am the divine (I am good).

At this point, I knew that some sort of transformation was going on within me. I wasn't sure what to make of it. I needed to find answers. It seemed spiritual to me, so I decided to contact the priest at a church in my neighbourhood and had a conversation with him. I told him what I was experiencing and he first asked me if I was under the influence of drugs or alcohol. I replied that I was not and that what I was experiencing felt real. Then he told me that I had had an epiphany, a spiritual awakening. He also mentioned that it is heard of but not very common. I was blessed and that I should follow it without any resistance. So I took his advice and had no resistance to what was happening and allowed it to continue. From that day forward, my sense of awareness and understanding has reached levels that I could not even imagine. My way of being, thinking, and being with others has been like no other. I completed a 180-degree turn. (Completing a 360 degree turn will place you in the same spot where you started).

As the words came to me on December 4, 2006, till this day I am living life full of love, compassion, peace, and understanding. There's nothing more fulfilling in life than being at peace with yourself and others. Each and every day, you spend more time with yourself than anyone else. You will go to sleep and wake up in the morning in the presence of yourself, more than with anyone else. So it is crucial that you are able to respect and love yourself with good thoughts and intentions.

On any given day, no matter how far you go or where you are, there you are. You cannot run away from your shadow; it goes with you, accompanied by your thoughts.

Thoughts and Expressions

Embrace and love one another, for we are all connected to one.

The choices you make and the attitude you have represents you entirely and no one else.

To find true love, one must experience and feel it within before they can truly feel it and experience it with another.

If you live your past in the present, it will become your future.

Having courage and taking responsibility for our own lives will make the world a better place.

We are all unique in our own way; let's set a good example of ourselves and follow it with grace.

If you live, think, and bring up issues of your past in the present, it will become your future.

We pass on and teach what we know.

The less you take things personally, the stronger you become

When you stop being tough, you gain the power and control to just be you.

Do not allow anyone to destroy your dreams. All dreams are possible if you take action and believe in your dreams.

Do not allow anyone to define who you truly are.

There will always be challenges in life. If we simply had all the answers, life would be boring.

NOTES FOR CHAPTER 2

Chapter Three
The Passage of Life to Peace and Freedom

Is your life on a path of peace and freedom? Knowing your life right now, and with the thoughts and experiences that have occurred in your life and how you are feeling, can you truly say to yourself, "When my time comes will I go in peace"? If the answer is *no* to either of these questions, then we have some work to do. There has to be an understanding to live a life of peace and freedom, and one must do the work *now* in order to rest in peace. I had a best friend from my past who died and wasn't prepared to die. He hadn't completed all that he desired to do in life to move on to his next life. During his living years, he was too preoccupied with serving everyone else's needs but his own, worrying more about other people's expectations and giving them the power to control his life. He had dreams that he didn't fulfill. Let's not be mistaken, I feel it is very important to serve others in this world who are in need, but it is also important to fulfill our dreams and heart's desires. We have been given life, so it's up to us to *live it now!* He was given three months to live, once he knew he had lung cancer. He died three months to the day from when he learned of the cancer. He was sixty-four. It was very painful to see my best friend in his last dying days unprepared and not ready to move on. He was upset, afraid, and frustrated because he knew his time was near.

Every direction we take in life and everything we do will sooner or later lead us to death. We have come into this world with nothing, and we leave with nothing. Let's not get so caught up in life with all the materialistic things that surround us. Don't get me wrong; we have an opportunity to enjoy and experience the wonderful things that life has to offer, but we mustn't use them to define us and control our life. At the end, we leave it all behind because we don't own it. I've yet to experience a funeral where anyone who has passed on has been able to take all their earthly possessions with them. Nothing goes with you; everything remains. What you do take with you is everything you stored in your *heart*, for the spirit never dies! If you want to have a life full of riches, invest in your heart. We must reflect now and prepare ourselves for a path in life of peace and freedom. To follow this path we need to free ourselves, so we're able to rest in peace. We must start *being* as we're set out to be in the beginning of life, as wonderful beautiful human beings, and stop getting caught up in just *doing!* Life's too short!

I have been very fortunate in my lifetime to meet a wonderful ninety-five year-old woman named Mary Scott. During our conversations, she spoke about her niece, who was forty-seven years of age at the time. Her niece was concerned about dying. Mary replied, "When you're my age, you don't mind dying." It's a wonderful statement to hear, and I would say that, knowing Mary over time and looking at the smile on her face, she has lived a life fulfilled. I have had many conversations with Mary. I found through conversations with her that she was able to share with me a wealth of knowledge reflecting her experiences. So I took the conversations seriously. It takes a journey of time in life to understand a *way of life.* Because she has been living life twice as long as I have, I thought I would pay special attention to the words she spoke.

I once asked, "Mary, after all these years, ninety-five years and counting, you still have a wonderful smile. You would think after all these years your smile would be worn out. What has kept you smiling all these years?" Her response was, "In life you must do well and do well to others. You can't just take in life; you must also be able to give back, because you live with everything you do, so by doing good and doing good to others you're able to live with yourself. You have to live life in a positive way and not be so negative. You hear people sometimes complaining about everything; they whine and complain about this and that, finding something wrong with this or that, so I push them aside. They're not bad people. I just choose not to be a part of it."

As Mary has taken responsibility for her life, so must we seek a desire and a way of living, so we too can live a life full of peace and freedom. You need to decide in your life right *now* if you want to live a full life that has been given, so at the end of your physical life you're able to truly rest in peace.

What will follow as you read on is an understanding and an awareness that is crucial. It is important to comprehend and understand it to have a life full of peace and freedom. The choice is entirely yours. You can choose, as I did, to take the responsibility, build up the courage and determination to have a peaceful, fulfilling life full of freedom, and live your life to the fullest, or you can continue to inherit the pain, misery, loneliness, and the fears that have kept you still in life, a life waiting to be lived.

There is one of two paths to choose in life—no others. I had a conversation with middle-aged woman who had experienced a past of abuse, both physical and emotional, and she was trying to find reason and answers to her pain. During our conversation, she brought up a thought. She said, ``I have been in this place of my life for the longest time, and I know no other way. I am too afraid and don't know which way to go. If I choose another way, it would scare me because I know no other way, and it may not be the right path.'' I explained to her that in life there are only two choices. If the path you are on has not provided peace and harmony in your life, then you need to act on and do the opposite of what you have been doing. There is no other way or choice. You decide one path or the other.

I can assure you that this process will not be easy but you must ask yourself, "Do I want to continue living life the way I have been and maintain the same results, create worse results, just living day by day, not progressing or enjoying life to the fullest, living to just breathe, a life spent wasting life? Or do I truly want to live the life that has been given to me so I can start the process to live life *now?*"

From my experience, the process and the understanding of the following four steps I followed, has helped me create a passage to my peace and freedom. I discovered this process on my own and realized that it was the key to my freedom. If you feel trapped and you don't know what to do (just like my situation on December 4, 2006), then this is your key;

It took me forty-five years to figure this out, and I did it. So if I could do it, so can you. By following these four steps, you too will be given a passage to a life of peace and freedom you can't even imagine, feeling fully alive and awake! But I caution: Do not lose sight. Stay on course. Don't get sidetracked. Focus on your will and courage, not on your fear and uncertainty to proceed. Fear will only keep you still! Avoid any negativity to all distorted words and thoughts. Do not create resistance to this process, and keep your feet away from following evil. No matter how hard it may be, allow this process to penetrate deep within your heart and mind, for this understanding will bring life and health to you and anyone who chooses to understand and follow it. This is your key to a life so fulfilled you will live it as you were set out to do—to the fullest in every way!

My True Understanding and Experience to a Life of Peace and Freedom

First— Being Understanding

Using the will and responsibility to develop an understanding of the experiences in your life is very crucial in this first step. You must have tolerance and find reason and truth about what has happened in your past. As painful as it may be, this is part of the process in order to move on. As I experienced in the early stages of this first step (understanding), I asked myself, "Why am I in this position, and why has this happened to me?" I reflected and analyzed my experiences, then started to realize that the pain that was inflicted on me was the pain that the other person was feeling. By having the tolerance and creating an open mind, I was able to find truth and reason to what happened in my life. I went back to family history and explored the relationships among my family members.

My father had a very similar relationship with his father as he had with me. He taught me what he knew through the experiences and teachings of his father. I then came to a conclusion by finding truth. I had inherited my father's pain and issues from his relationship with his father. In understanding this truth, I sympathized with him and realized at a young age (sixteen) that it had nothing to do with me. He was fighting his own battles and decided to take others with him along the way. I realized through study and observation that this inheritance of past life issues and experiences went back several generations.

After taking responsibility for my own life by being more understanding and compassionate, I started the process of letting go of something that had been passed on to me at a very young age. I chose a different path. I have believed since then that, "if it isn't yours, then don't take ownership of it." In conversations with others, I have discovered that letting go of past conflict and pain was a major roadblock in their lives. Some results would lead to others feeling hurt, angry, resentful, and fearful, having low self-esteem, and resenting the idea of forgiving the ones who hurt them, leaving them in a place in life that limited their way of being. Having these roadblocks and obstacles in their past brought into their present a limited "way of being" with others authentically.

Let's use my father's example in the relationship he had with his father. The experience and relationship my father had with his father (male to male) had a direct impact on the relationships he had with other males (including myself). My father's mother, on the other hand, had a different relationship with my father. They had a closer relationship with each other. She was more expressive, caring, and demonstrated more affection towards him. The experience and relationship my father had with his mother (male to female) had a similar and direct impact on the relationship he has had with my mother and sister.

One of the greatest influences in our life is our parents. The male role played by the father and the female role played by the mother have great influence on the relationships we have with other males and females in our lives. Aside from our parental teachings (the inner family circle) as our first teachers, we learn and become influenced by others around us. For example, our first-grade teachers and classmates have a great influence on our way of learning and way of being in the early stages of our lives. We build a relationship and experiences with our first-grade teachers and classmates. We then make a comparison with our first teachers—our parents. Through my first teachings (my parents) in the early stages of my childhood, up to the age of six, I was told that I was not smart enough to achieve anything. Having this understanding at the age of six, I entered into grade one and took my understanding into the classroom. Through the school year in grade one, my home environment, and because of the experiences I was dealing with, I became easily distracted and had difficulty learning. I also had conflict with fellow students. The result was that I failed and had to repeat grade one. This confirmed my first teachings (my parents) and made me believe that I was not smart or capable enough.

My twin sister, also in grade one in the same year, advanced to grade two. It was a devastating experience at that age. For years, this affected every aspect of my life—my sense of worth, self-esteem, and way of being as a child. At a young age, it doesn't take much to be devastated and hurt. As young children, we filter and experience everything good and bad. You only need to be told once by anyone who has had a great influence on you to make you believe something.

I will stress again that it is prudent to take the action and the responsibility to find reason and truth from your past. Once you know the actual truth, you will then have more clarity so you're able to start the process of *letting go!* Understanding this first important step will bring you closer to a life of peace and freedom.

Second—Being Compassionate

In order to be compassionate, you need to first have an understanding. You cannot forgive if you're not compassionate. By having an understanding you will see the full picture and make a true assessment of your experience and involvement with anyone who has hurt you. As the saying goes, "Knowing the truth will set you free." From my experience, I discovered that by putting myself in the other person's shoes to find truth and reason enabled me to understand their role and involvement, therefore focusing more on placing my thoughts and energy on resolution and not on being the victim. If we focus on being the victim or blame the other, we lose the desire to find a resolution. Without seeing the whole picture, we become one sided, and the entire truth becomes *distorted!* As I mentioned earlier, it is very important to eliminate the fear within you in order to proceed. Fear will be a major obstacle to overcome in order to complete all four important steps. Since fear is one of the emotions used to control us, we need to eliminate the fear within us in order to move on.

There is a saying, "He who instills fear in others has feared himself." There will come a time where you may have to come face to face with the individual or individuals who have done wrong to you or created pain in your life. By holding onto the fear, you may feel powerless or intimidated to deal by the individuals and circumstances that have held you back in life.

I want you to understand that *fear* is an acronym: *false evidence that appears real*. It's an illusion of the truth. Fear is a weakness. You need to have control over fear, or fear will have control over you. You give what you receive and what you have. In my situation, by being compassionate, I realized that what my father received from his father was what he gave to me. This is true of people in general: they give what they have received and experienced from others. It's a way of justifying the way they feel. You're able to see this, for example, in an individual who is angry, miserable, and upset. The way they feel is the way they want others to feel: angry, miserable, and upset. They do what it takes to make others feel the way they do. An individual, on the other hand, who is outgoing and cheerful, will make others feel the same way. When you take full responsibility and control over your own life, you gain the full power to be who you truly are—a wonderful, beautiful human being. Being compassionate is feeling for the other in having a true understanding of their character and their circumstances and knowing where all of it has originated from. You will see by first having an understanding, and by being compassionate, that what happened to you *never originated from you, It was passed on to you!*

Third—Being Forgiving

To follow the process of forgiving, one must be understanding and compassionate. It is very difficult to forgive someone if there is no understanding and compassion. Individuals will spend a lifetime fighting forgiveness and resisting it because they have a hard time letting go of issues, conflict, and circumstances that have set in with themselves and others. They will play the role of the victim, have resentment, anger, and guilt connected to their experiences with others. You need to understand that by forgiving someone, you release *yourself* from the pain and misery that the other has given. You're doing it for yourself. You are not giving in, lowering your standards, or making the other person look good. You're letting go and leaving it behind.

As a child, you don't have many options or choices in your *way of life*. As an adult, you have the power to define who you want to be. You also have the power to choose who you will have in your life and how to deal with them. It's entirely up to you. But if you continue to hold onto past pain and issues that have come from others, they will always be a part of your life because you haven't let go. I believe; in order to move forward in life and have a life full of peace, you must be able to forgive anyone who has made any mistakes, hurt you or done any wrong to you. You must also forgive yourself for any mistakes that you've made in your life, any pain you put yourself and others through, and any wrong you've done to yourself and others.

By taking the blame and responsibility in our lives, the person we find most difficulty to forgive is ourselves. You need to let it go because, if you don't, it will always be attached to you. You will inherit it and share it with others. You must be fair to yourself and release what isn't yours. You have done up to now what you could with what you experienced and what you have learned in life. You made mistakes along the way; that's okay. We all make mistakes from time to time and we are far from perfect. Making mistakes is part of the learning process. I don't know of anyone who hasn't made a mistake in his or her life. We can all agree, if we had all the answers to life and made no mistakes, life would be pretty boring. It's important to reflect on the mistakes that we've made in our lives, by taking responsibility, and learning from them so history does not repeat itself. You cannot move forward if you continue to make the same mistakes.

My direct experience to this is what happened on December 4, 2006, (which I described in reference to chapter I.) I forgave myself for the pain that I put myself and others through. By doing this, I set myself free! Taking things personally from others can create a barrier to forgiving as well. Don't take it so personally. If a person is upset and they're lashing out at you, chances are they're lashing out at themselves. People in general give what they receive and receive what they give, so don't take it so personally. *It's not about you!* Not taking things personally and finding reason is much easier said than done. You're not being fair to yourself by taking it personally. You can only take responsibility for your own actions, words, and way of being. Understanding this important step will give you the power and control to be you. The way you represent yourself is how others will perceive and respond to you. The power and result of forgiveness is freedom!

Fourth—Being Loving

Love is sacred and the most important ingredient in life. It is the greatest nourishment to the soul. Without love, life is hopeless. Human beings fall into despair and lose hope when they're not loved or feeling loved. They feel lonely and isolated. Our feelings and needs toward love in our adult lives are the same needs as when we were children. It is just as important. We search for love as adults, just as we did as children. When pain enters our life, love can be replaced by other emotions, such as hate, anger, resentment, pity, hopelessness, lack of self-worth, and so forth. The individual loses site of his original core way of being—a wonderful, beautiful human being. We must not lose sight of the fact that love will prevail, love will conquer all, and true love lies within us. It will always stand the test of time.

I feel that love is the most important and most powerful emotion of all. It is also the greatest weapon of all. You can take your worst enemy and have them drop before you with tenderness and love. Loving others and including yourself for any hurt or wrongdoing is extremely powerful. There is more purpose and power in loving for one's life than being hurtful. When one loves within and towards others, that person is demonstrating full control in his or her life.

A true winner in any battle is the one who avoids violent confrontation and demonstrates a will to love and understanding. I see these individuals as true leaders and winners in our society. They set a great example for us on the definition of humanity and their roles as wonderful, beautiful human beings. Throughout history, we have witnessed individuals such as Gandhi, Mother Teresa, and others who have set this example. Love and forgiveness are closely linked and feed off each other. Having an understanding, being compassionate and also forgiving are acts of love. There is a saying, "if you truly love someone, you must set them free." There may come a time in our lives where we need to set someone free, (including ourselves for any mistakes or wrongdoing in our lives). This may occur when someone has hurt us in life or someone in a relationship has chosen to move on and take a different path. It isn't an easy task, but it is an important step for one's freedom. We need to make tough decisions at times, when we have no choice but to free ourselves from certain people.

As Mary Scott once told me, "They're not bad people. I just choose to go around them and not to be a part of it." We need to accept that some individuals, whether they are friends, family, or close acquaintances, may always remain as they are and choose not to change for the better or take full responsibility for their lives. Some may continue being negative, hurtful, judgmental, blaming, and so forth. You need to be careful with such individuals, because people who are miserable enjoy the company of others who are also miserable. We have the power to choose not be a part of it and simply work around it. We still need to do our part and not dislike such individuals, just have the power within us to forgive them and let them go. As wonderful, beautiful human beings, it's in our nature to love and to be loved.

When Is It Going to End?

We're born and we experience and learn through others who have come into our lives. They teach us what they have learned and experienced in their lives. It goes on from generation to generation, family to family, relationship to relationship. The pattern and the consistency of the actions and intentions are all too similar from past life experiences. So when is the pattern going to stop, and when will there be change?

History seems to repeat itself time and time again. Life experiences and circumstances don't change, so when will someone have the courage to make the changes so history does not repeat itself? Without change, everything remains the same. If history repeats itself, there can be no change. If we take action, responsibility, and make changes from our past, our future will change. You see, if you bring back history, circumstances, and issues and act on them in the same manner with no change in the present moment, it will then become your future, where again history will repeat itself.

It is simple to understand an individual's way of being. You are who you are from your life experiences. By taking personal responsibility for your life and finding truth and reason in your past, you will discover who you truly are. You will then have the power to break the cycle and stop history from repeating itself.

Thoughts and expressions

We will all endure pain at some point in our lives. The best cure is understanding, compassion, forgiveness, and love.

Embrace love, for love will embrace you.

Let's unite our wings together to create a united force, so we can carry on to our wings every living spirit in need. Let us do this with grace.

When the heart needs strength and care, give it as much love as you can, for you only have one incredible heart.

In life, love is the greatest of all, for without it life is lonely, meaningless, and hopeless.

You cannot give what you do not have.

The beginning of every blessing day in life is a new beginning to life.

Set a steady pace, look forward, and not back, for it has passed.

Having passion, affection, love, and romance in one's heart, the time and place is always perfect.

The greatest pain of all comes straight from the heart. The best treatment is unconditional love.

Place a rope upon the heavens and hold on tight, for the only place to go is up.

Wherever you go, whatever you do, there you are.

Life is like playing sports: the more you practice and commit to life, the better life gets.

When a difficult time appears in life, one must reflect, have faith, avoid evil, and stay the proper course to keep standing.

Simplify your approach in life, don't complicate it. Life is not that complicated. The mathematics to life is: 10 percent of life is what happens to you, and 90 percent is how you react to it.

If you don't deal with the issues that you're faced with in your life and don't take responsibility for them, the person who will suffer most is you.

Time will pass, but memories will remain.

The four important words to peace and freedom in one's life are these: Understanding, compassion, forgiveness, and love.

Go everywhere and do everything with all your heart.

There is nothing more fulfilling than being at peace with yourself.

You get what you give.

YOU HAVE COME TO THE "HEART" OF THIS BOOK

The following are actual words, ideas, and understandings that came to my realization during the time of my epiphany and my spiritual awakening. Go into this slowly and take your time to reflect.

Free at Last—I have served My Time

It is time to move on and leave behind my imprisoned life. A life that had no direction, purpose, meaning, or light; a time in not knowing, just breathing. It is time to move on to a passage and journey that is as clear as the sun. A sense of all good energy flowing through me to live life and experience it to the *fullest*, for my heart and soul has awakened truthfully to everything good. Free of all bad and free of all fear. *Free at last!*

Day by Day

Day by day, step by step, time by time, we inch forward through what we know and what we have seen, learned, and experienced to continue our journey, a journey to reach a resting place we hope to call Heaven. May you find the right passage and journey in your life so you can truly R.I.P.—rest in peace.

The Light of Life Given or Taken Away

Living in the light, life is bright and meaningful with no end in sight.

Living in darkness, life becomes hopeless and lifeless.

Choosing your path in life will create the way, for you can choose to live in the light or live in darkness.

Awaken Me

Awaken me from this bad dream I am having. Bring in the light so I can wake up and see. Make some noise. Please talk to me. I need to wake up.

I have Awakened

I have awakened to the voice of my heart. All I can hear are beautiful words and thoughts. All I can feel is peaceful, warm, and compassionate with love and understanding, feeling and understanding in the presence of others. All I can see is a warm, bright light that seems endless insight, a light that has brightened my heart and life. For my heart has seen no light for a very long time. I have awakened. The light is strong and bright and my path is clear, for I have awakened from a bad dream.

Life Given

Life given is a precious gift that should not be taken for granted, for as it is given, it can also be taken away with a lack of understanding at times for the reasons not knowing why, so indulge in the life given for it is a precious gift.

Human Plant

The human plant is very unique and very complex. It is easy to care for but hard to maintain. To care for the human plant, one must supply abundant light, water, nourishment, wholesome food, and oxygen. One must give it enough space so it can grow and flourish and enough soil so the roots can spread and absorb more nourishment and water. To be kind to your plant also works. Talk to it in a kind and gentle way. Always handle your human plant with care. To destroy the human plant, simply do the opposite. Use pesticide, no water, no light, no care, no food, do not treat it with love, abuse it, abandoned it, and you will destroy it.

The Eyes of the Child within Us

Little child, shine your beautiful eyes upon me. Teach me what you feel. Bring out the little, sweet child within me. Teach me how to sing, love, play, dance, learn and live. Connect me to your source. It has been a very long time since I have been back there. I don't want to take life as seriously as I have; I just want to go back in time as a little child and live life and feel just like you.

Painful, Bleeding Heart

Why do you continue to bleed? Come forward and seek treatment; bandage your wound to stop the bleeding. Follow the treatment, for you can heal. Treat and condition it with love to what it once was. Slowly start the process of your treatment to make it strong, for you only have one incredible *heart!*

You're Choice

The choice is yours. You can choose to;

- Live or die
- Be happy or sad
- Live in light or live in darkness
- Take responsibility for your life or blame others
- Set a good or bad example for yourself
- Love or hate
- Give unconditionally or always take
- Heal your pain or create more pain
- Think and feel the way you want to

At the start of every blessing day given, *it's your choice!* There is no in between.

What is Love?

Love is a simple word to say but can be complicated to understand. It can be misunderstood, confusing to understand, very complex to understand; it can be known or not known at all. What is love you may ask? I love this; house, car, bike, table, picture, etc. (object), or I hate it. I love; my mother, father, friend, husband, wife, child, bird, cat, dog, etc. (human or living thing), or I hate it. So what is love?

Love is an understanding and a beautiful feeling about you and your heart's feelings. It is feeling good and having a happy inner connection with you, feeling from the inside-out good and content. There is no hate, judgment, ratings towards it, or middle grounds (I feel in love or I don't feel in love), etc. You are inspired when in love with everything because it is an inner spirit (in-spirit) that makes the connection with you. It is your heart that truly knows the incredible, wonderful connection you have with yourself and everything else around you. Any other thoughts, beliefs, distractions, misconceptions, or sayings to the word *love*, means nothing more.

You cannot hear, taste, smell, see, or touch if you don't use your ears, tongue, nose, eyes, or hands. You cannot love or know love unless you go to and feel from your......*heart*.

The Actor

The actor lives in many of us. The actor will wake up in the morning, wash up, and put on an outfit (costume), and head out into the world (on stage) and perform. Actors' outfits will vary each day as well as the performance. At the end of their performance (day), they take off their outfit (costume), and they then become in tune with the real performer, the real actor who is underneath the costume, makeup, or mask they're wearing and see that what they had to perform to or act was just an act.

Blaming

Blaming is a simple way of handing over responsibility to someone else. In the person's mind, it's an easy way out. When you point one finger at someone else, three fingers point at you. The blamer just passes it on to someone else and resolves nothing. If every single person took responsibility for himself or herself, we would not have as much crime, violence, hunger, corruption, pain, misery, divorces, misunderstandings, etc. We would simply do what it takes to make it good. It is everyone's responsibility, not another's.

In My Box

I sit here all alone in my box. I see nothing around me, only four walls with the scriptures and the words written all over them. I see nothing else but the words that I know are in this box. If only I have the courage and strength to climb over the walls, I will see anything else, but I find it comfortable here. It would scare me if I had to go. It's all I know, living in my box...We are all able minded—open your mind, climb out of your box.

Tears of Many Faces

Life experiences and life feelings set in, and then tears appear. Each and every expression is unique. Tears appear on many occasions. At times, when we are happy, sad, lonely, in physical or emotional pain, lost, found; at times when loved ones come into our lives or when loved ones are gone. Tears appear when we're born. Tears appear no more when we're gone.

Tears are liquid expressions of your life and life feelings.

Stars

Look into the stars, for you are not alone. There is one star that you can call your own.

The Adult

The adult has been developed through life experiences. From the beginning, the child is born with good, clear conscience, no experience, and little feelings and emotions. Feelings and emotions are not fully developed until later on.

A newborn is never born badly. What defines a newborn's personality and way of being is its experiences and thoughts towards their teachings and upbringing in its life. The newborn is not born with bad feelings, good or bad thoughts, judgments or liking or hating; a newborn is drawn into it. For example, if parents are abusive or they're alcoholics or take drugs and hate, newborns are drawn and exposed to it. If parents have an unstable lifestyle, kids are drawn into and exposed to it. If parents are caring, loving, and expressive in a decent way, kids are drawn into and exposed to it. In the child's first five to ten years of life, the biggest influence in their lives is their parents. It's the world the kids know. They develop their way of being by what they see, hear, experience, and feel. By adulthood, they are formed through what they have seen at home and from what they have seen and experienced in the outside world. They then become responsible in directing and controlling their own lives. At the end, a good life in all categories is no mistake. Below are some powerful guidelines to follow to have a great life;

- Do not judge.
- Be kind and loving towards yourself and others every day.
- What you give to the universe, you will receive back. For example, give love and the universe will give it back. Give resentment and hate and you will get it back in return.
- Give unconditionally.
- Take responsibility for your life.
- Do well to others.
- Don't blame everyone else.
- Listen and feel from your heart.
- Live and explore outside your comfort zone.
- Find truth and reason towards your thoughts.
- Forgive everyone, including yourself for any pain given or any wrongdoing.
- Stay the course of positive thinking and avoid negativity.

Courage

Stand up and fight, not in a physical way but in a mental way (using the mind). The mind is more powerful than the physical self. In a circus, the lion trainer has control of the show by using only his mind, not his physical strength. By physical strength, the lion would win with no contest. Courage starts and ends by using a strong mind, directing it to the right path. A weak mind will never win. It would have to be reconditioned. Your mind drives your physical being. Without your mind, you cannot move, breathe, think, feel, see, and so forth, nor can you function. You're mind driven in a positive way with good thoughts and intentions, eliminating fear will win the title of courage. The strongest mind in all *positive* ways, combined with a heart that is both united and driven to have courage, always wins. A strong mindset that is driven in a negative way may have courage but at the end will always lose.

The Complainer

If you have everything in your life and you're not content and you always complain, your life isn't fulfilled. Something is missing.

The Shopaholic

If you continually shop, buying things that you need but are still looking for more, you're not shopping at the right place. The place you need to search is within your heart. All your shopping needs and satisfactions are there.

Celebrate Life

Celebrate the everlasting life. It is within us all. As you reflect on your life, reach into your heart and touch the ones you love, for they have come and gone.

The Mind

A weak mind will create a weak body.

A strong mind will create a determined, strong-willed body.

A weak mind will create a weak unfulfilling life, full of misguided and distorted thoughts.

A strong mind will create a determined life, full of good thinking, positive direction, love, wealth, self-contentment, and the enjoyment of people and life.

Your way of thinking will have a great impact on your health and your way of being in life.

High and low—fast and slow

High energy—low energy

Fast energy—slow energy

Life energy is fast and slow, high and low. Their must be stability in the energy of your life; to have a balance

Stay in Touch

Stay in touch with yourself. See within and all around you. Experience the feelings and emotions that set in. Reflect with sense and understanding, and set an example of yourself. Represent yourself with good intentions; take two steps back to see two steps forward. Don't misrepresent yourself. Work on your physical, spiritual, and mental self. Always be true to yourself and others in your life.

Your Life—Your Computer

Your way of being in life and your mind works like your computer. You need an anti-virus program to protect your hard drive (mind) from any viruses (bad unwanted thoughts), so your computer (mind) works efficiently and effectively. Pop-ups and viruses appear (distorted unwanted thoughts). Anti-virus programs will remove them (leaving good thoughts in place). Download and store in your computer (mind) what is helpful (positive thinking). Delete unwanted material (distorted and negative thoughts). You need to constantly upgrade your software (knowledge and information) to meet the demands that are required (in your life). If you don't upgrade your computer (mind), your computer (mind) becomes outdated.

You Can Run but You Can't Hide

No matter how far and for as long as you go, you will never run away from your shadow and your mind. So deal with it, because if you don't, your thoughts will always be there until you deal with them.

United As One—United We Stand

On the surface, we appear to be un-united and different, but it is the inner being that is all the same, all coming from the same source, and nothing is different—the inner source and connection that we all have with the infinite spirit.

Look Into Your Eyes

(Go slowly into this and take your time).

Look into your life. What do you see? Look into your eyes. What have they seen? Filter through your eyes. Where have they been? Register through your mind. What does it think? From your eyes and your mind, feel from the heart. What do you feel?

Life of a Boomerang

Write on the boomerang the words and the message that you want to send out. Chances are the same message will come back to you, for this is the life of a boomerang—it comes back to you.

Living Life Unlimited

Living a limited life will limit you from life. You will simply put a cap on your life. If you want to live life unlimited, you have to stop limiting yourself, step outside of your comfort zone, explore, and experience a life that has no limits. There is no limit to numbers; there's no limit to the sky. There is no limit to life, for life is everlasting.

Danger! Keep out!

Don't come here; it's a bad place to be. Keep out! I know you would like to take me out of danger, but I've been here long enough to know the game. You don't know, so please stay out, or you will be a player like me, if you're not careful, because you see, it's like a cage, once you're in it, it's hard to get out. It's dangerous! Keep out!

How have you been?

How have you been? The answer is simple. Filter the question from your mind to your heart. The answer lies within your heart.

The Human Race

The human race with your legs in motion, where are you racing to? Seems kind of confusing at times, because the race should be moving in one direction, but I see this human race going in different directions. You need to follow the right path, if you're going to win the race. Remember, you only have so much time to finish. So stay on track, follow your heart feelings and instincts, and you will find the finish line and then claim your prize.

W.I.N.G.S.

Wind

In

Natures

Graceful

Spirit

Help me use my wings so I can fly above and meet with you and your angels. Let us unite our wings together, so we can create a united force, so we can carry on to our wings every living spirit in need. Let us do this with grace.

Being Institutionalized

We become institutionalized through our mind from past experiences that set us up for where we are. We follow certain rules and regulations that at times limit us from our full potential. For example, when working in a factory and being told what to do, or as a child limiting experiences—don't do this, don't do that, you're not capable, not good enough, and so forth, building a negative wall of thoughts and energy as you go on in life. You also experience the fear that is given to control you. You create a narrow path in life of limitations, a false belief and way of being, feeling institutionalized (imprisoned).

Flight 007—Destination: Freedom

This is the last call for flight 007. Everyone departing on flight 007 please board the plane and leave your baggage behind. You may bring on board all your positive thinking, good intentions, smiles, warm expressions, and all good known to mankind. For this flight's destination is freedom.

Ocean Waters

Waters of abundance wash ashore before me. Show me your strength, cleanse me. Dry me with the presence of your wind and sun, blend me into the sand and soil. Supply me the essence of the beauty and life you bring to me, and all your fellow creatures. As the sun starts to disappear over the blue horizon and into a beautiful sunset, continue to wash to shore all before me and give hope, so we can connect in the morning and go on our journey another day.

Radiant Sun

Supply me the abundance of your source, for without it there is no life. Warm my soul and body with your gentle flow of rays. Bring to me all the light that you can to lighten my life and give me energy. Nourish me and all living things that depend on you, for without your presence there would be no life.

Crystal Eyes

Draw upon me your inner sparkle. Reflect all the wonderful colors through your crystal eyes, for I can see through them clearly, all the goodness you possess.

In Line With Mind and Spirit

Mind-spirit works together, creating all good thoughts and intentions, eliminating false beliefs and distorted thoughts.

Fear

Who needs courage if you have no fear?

Stop!

Stop:
- Stop the emotional and physical pain.
- Stop inheriting other people's pain as your responsibility.
- Stop hating life and everything in it.
- Stop hating yourself and others.
- Stop making up untrue stories and beliefs.
- Stop the abuse and violence.
- Stop judging.
- Stop taking from the universe.
- Stop your distorted thinking and negative thoughts.
- Stop making bad choices that only hurt you and others.
- Stop the fear in you.
- Stop living in darkness.
- Stop walking away and avoiding.
- Stop making the same mistakes!

- Stop blaming everyone else and not taking responsibility for yourself.
- Stop denying.
- Stop living in a closed environment with yourself.
- Stop wasting time.
  S T O P!!!

Start!

Start:
- Start to love yourself and then others.
- Start to believe in the truth and the power of good intentions and good thoughts towards mankind.
- Start giving back to the universe.
- Start taking responsibility for yourself.
- Start being and thinking positive.
- Start making good choices.
- Start living life.
- Start aligning your mind with your heart.
- Start exercising.
- Start connecting to and improving your physical, mental, and spiritual self.

- Start opening your eyes—the window to your soul, to the vast universe around you.
- Start living from the heart.
- Start respecting yourself and then others.
- Start living the wonderful child you are (within).
- Start living life *now!*
  Start!

Give It Up!

Give it up! You don't own it, nor are you responsible for someone else's pain. It was never yours to begin with, so give it up! Accept it, forgive, and understand it, and give it up! Take ownership of who you truly are: *a wonderful, beautiful human being!*

Who Says?

- Who says you can't?
- Who says you will fail?
- Who says you're not smart enough?
- Who says you don't have it in you?
- Who says that it will never happen to you?

- Who says you're no good?
- Who says it isn't possible?
- Who says because they didn't succeed what makes you think you will?
- Who says this is as good as it gets?

He or she who says you can't has been lying to you all along, because the truth of the matter is, *you can!* If you don't achieve it or succeed, at least you've tried. You'll never know unless you try. Simply saying you can't is only an excuse. The will and determination will sooner or later get you there.

Live in the Moment

Live in the moment *now!* Bless the past and let it go, for it has gone. Be optimistic and look to the future for what it has in stored for you.

You

Someone's opinion of you and their reality should not define who you truly are.

Never Stop!

Never stop learning, loving, caring, giving, understanding, living, laughing, extending friendship, feeling, having compassion, giving affection, sharing, observing, embracing, listening, smiling, sharing intimacy, spreading peace, and achieving good—*never stop living now!*

When In Love

When two are in love, both become as one, like two ice cubes melting together, or two bodies becoming as one. Love=2 into 1.

The Passage of Life

The past is history

The present is the *now* reality

The future is unknown and a mystery.

Faith and hope will create the path to victory.

If You Don't

If you don't deal with and take responsibility for the issues that are holding you still in life, the person who will suffer most is you.

Mind and Body

The mind will make you or break you. The body is innocent. It is the mind that does to the body. You bring everything upon you by the energy force you give out and the thoughts you create and take in.

Fear

Fear will paralyze you. It will limit you. Eliminate it, or it will eliminate your place in life and life's experiences. It will make you still!

Desire to Have and Achieve

Having a desire and being inspired to achieve something is like falling in love. The energy is so powerful that you need to have it in your life. Being motivated with your heart's inspiration is a very powerful energy to have. You become very driven. Can you recall the feeling of falling in love? The feeling is so strong that you must be with that person. The desire to have and achieve is the same feeling towards life. Creating that desire will drive you no matter what circumstances come your way. The greatest accomplishments in life have been achieved through this understanding.

Life is Like a Hotel

When you enter into life, it's like checking into a hotel. You check in and are able to enjoy all the features the hotel has to offer. Depending on where you like to stay, some hotels are more appealing than others with higher standards and more to offer. Then there comes a time when you have to check out, so others can check in, allowing them to follow the same process. So enjoy your stay, because sooner or later, you will have to check out.

Passion

In having passion, affection, love, and romance in one's heart, the times and places are always perfect.

Needing in Life

A child is always looking for recognition and attention. They are always leaving their trail behind. A handprint here, a toy there, clothes in the way, yelling and screaming, and a mess everywhere. As adults, we also crave recognition and attention for who we are. We have always felt a need to be wanted, accepted, and loved, to be able to leave a trail.

Question frequently asked:

How is life treating you?

The answer all depends on your attitude to life and how you are treating life.

Making an Affirmation with Yourself

I have been given another day, and today I will do the best that I can with what I have and what I know. I will to do a little better today than yesterday, and I will accept that I do not have control over everything. I will create no resistance to my day and allow the process to happen.

A Formula to an Unfulfilled and Unhappy Life

You are born into this life and experience the things that happen to you. You journey a life to experience the positive and negative things in life. You put all your energy and emphasis on the pain, any wrongdoing and misery that have entered your life, and you choose to own it. You are too comfortable to make other choices, because it is what you have come to accept and you focus on it. You are too afraid or lack the courage to take the responsibility to find reasons to give them up. You feel others deserve the negative experiences that you have been given, so you drag them into your life and become miserable and unhappy in doing so.

A Formula for a Fulfilled and Happy Life

You're born into this life and experience the things that happened to you in life. You journey in life to deal with the pain, any wrongdoing and misery that has entered your life. You build the courage by eliminating fear and decide to take responsibility without blaming others to find truth and reason. You choose a path in order to find resolution to your past, and you move on by letting go of it all. You become understanding, compassionate, forgiving, and loving towards yourself and others. You focus on being positive, giving, optimistic, and hopeful of your future to find reason to live.

NOTES FOR CHAPTER 3

Chapter Four
The Power of Your Word

The word is very powerful. The words you choose to speak are a self-representation of how you are feeling and being. You must have control and use caution when speaking, for a word can heal a wounded heart or it can destroy it. You are fully responsible for the words you speak. You must be in full control of your words at all times and take responsibility for the words you speak. You should acknowledge to others when your words are not appropriate and be fully accountable. The reactions and actions from others depend on your choices of words and how they are spoken.

By using our brains we are fortunate to be able to articulate our words and communicate our thoughts, feelings, expressions, emotions, intentions, and actions. Over the centuries, the power of the word has brought nations and their people both closer together and further apart. Through contact and communication, words have saved lives and destroyed them.

The mind and heart work together. Signals received in the mind are filtered through the heart. If words or communication come from the mind and are not filtered by the heart, or they don't align through heart and mind, the words and statements spoken are more of an illusion. The mind can play tricks if one isn't aware. Have you ever had a thought or believed something, only to find out later that it was not real or true? An old expression states, "a wise man will think before he speaks." By doing so you are not only thinking but you are also feeling out the situation before you speak. It is important to do this but at times it is difficult to achieve. We lose control and the power within us by speaking before we actually feel and think about what we need to say. Proper self-expression and self-representation are two of the most difficult things to do on a daily basis. Use caution and be aware when you involve our mind, emotions, and words you use when representing yourself to others. Depending on your thoughts, the words you choose and the way you represent yourself will either be self empowering or self defeating.

Emotions

From our natural way of being, our childhood, and into the present moment, we have developed our emotions through life experiences. Emotions are created through our way of thinking. The brain has been developed this way. Our thoughts and emotions that set in and how we react to them determines how we will be. There is a direct link between our thoughts and our emotions. For example, an experience has set in or something has just happened, and our mind processes the experience, which creates an emotion. If the experience brings happiness and joy, our thoughts and emotions are expressed in the same way. If the experience brings abuse and pain, our thoughts and emotions may reflect anger and sorrow. Some emotions that we may have experienced and can relate to are:

Love   Remorse
Fear   Worry
Hatred   Regret

Embarrassment	Disgust
Guilt	Disappointment
Anger	Boredom
Pity	Envy
Pride	Curiosity
Rage	Excitement
Surprise	Depression
Suffering	Grief
Shame	Desire
Sadness	Ecstasy
Jealousy	Frustration
Gratitude	Anxiety
Interest	Happiness
Horror	Hostility
Empathy	Hope
Acceptance	Affection

Some facts about emotions

- Emotions come naturally and are a natural way of being in all of us.
- Emotions affect our way of being.
- Emotions are present in all relationships, including the relationship we have with ourselves.

- Emotions have an impact on our means of communication, our actions, and intentions.
- Emotions are expressed uniquely with each person by ways of visual and verbal expressions.
- Emotions are linked with our mind. The mind (brain) starts the process of our emotions.

Some myths about emotions:

- Emotions are not normal.
- Emotions cannot be trusted.
- Emotions should be ignored.
- Emotions are a sign of weakness.
- Emotions are not real.
- Emotions can't be controlled.
- Emotions are an exaggeration and made up.

Managing Emotions during Conflict and Avoiding Separation

Eleven constructive points to consider during conflict:

1. *Don't argue in a destructive and hurtful way.* You won't feel good about it, nor will you accomplish anything. You may lose

the power to negotiate your position and it won't make you look good.

2. *Be patient during conflict and listen.* If you want to be heard, be patient and listen first; you will have more clarity and understanding.

3. *Support and understand the other person's concerns and needs.* Chances are the other will do the same for you.

4. *Back off and take time out if necessary.* When emotions run high, it's time to take a walk. Let the other person know that you're not avoiding their concerns and that you're taking time out to reflect and regroup your thoughts. Give them a time frame when you'll be back to discuss the matter.

5. *It's not about being right or getting even.* Respect each other's opinion and play on the same team. It's not a competition, and if you make it so you will both lose!

6. *Control your anger.*
Avoid uncontrollable rage (blind rage). Take a deep breath. If anger is about to set in, take a time out, focus on your anger and find reasons why you are angry. Usually your anger has hidden issues that have not been resolved. Avoid uncontrollable rage in every sense of the word, the result can be *deadly*!

7. *Be positive and solution-orientated.*
Where there's a will there is a way. Being optimistic and having a positive outlook and the willpower, is a great way to find a solution.

8. *Don't bring up the past in a negative way.*
You can learn from your past. If you bring up your past in a negative way, it won't do you any favours. It will only set you back.

9. *Don't compare.*
We are all unique in our own ways. Comparing one another is taking away from the individual's unique-

ness. Appreciate and respect each other's roles in the relationship and each other's way of being. It's not a contest.

10. *Avoid separation by pulling towards each other.*
When the going gets tough, you weather the storm and you stick together to find a solution. You will be tested and challenged from time to time. Separating and not communicating will only bring misunderstanding, confusion, and loneliness, which can also lead to permanent separation.

11. *Use caution when you speak.*
Words have power. The words you choose can soothe the heart or they can be hurtful.

Our emotions at times can be difficult to control, let alone trying to control the emotions of others, especially during conflict. When you are dealing in conflict, slow down and manage your own emotions and actions. Stay in tune with yourself. Truly express your feelings to the others involved without offending them. Listen to the other person's feelings and observe his or her emotions. Be understanding and compassionate towards the other person; if you are, chances are the other person may sooner or later become the same way towards you. Fire added to fire will create more fire! Know when to take a time-out and request it to allow yourself time to calm down and reflect on your thoughts and emotions so you can continue with more clarity and understanding towards the situation and each other.

Anger and fear are common emotions that can set us back in life, if we allow them to. For example, a person expressing anger; trying to tell you something" (reaching out). Underneath the anger, if you listen and pay close attention, are hidden issues and concerns that need to be addressed or haven't been resolved. For most individuals, anger is most commonly used towards individuals who pose no threat. It is a way for individuals to release some pressure from themselves.

Another example of anger and fear: Anger and fear taken in—when someone receives it from another. For example; physical or verbal abuse, control, resentment, mistreatment, pain given from someone else, being hurt from a loved one, upset at themselves, and so forth. Anger and fear given out; feeling and experiencing all of the anger and fear one has take in is what they give out.

No one has the power to make anyone angry, unless we give them the power. Anger is an emotion that we can control, but first we need to deal with the underlying issues that haven't been resolved with understanding, compassion, forgiveness, and love. If there is no resolution, then anger becomes a bitter game in which we go back and forth, giving and receiving and receiving and giving anger to the conclusion: no one wins.

Thoughts and Expressions

It takes no effort to speak words. The effort is in the action and movement of your words spoken.

Life is like a boomerang. Write every thought and intention on it, toss it out, and it will come right back at you.

Perfection takes a lifetime to master, but even then we are not perfect.

Use caution when speaking your word, for the word has power.

Listen to the words of your heart, not the words of the mouth. Flourish and grow, for you are loved.

The words you speak are a representation of who you are and what you're being.

NOTES FOR CHAPTER 4

Chapter Five
Money without a Brain Has No Power

If you truly think about money, you may think that it has power. In truth, money has no power of its own. For example, we will just use a one-hundred dollar bill (note) in this case, although depending on investment or financial situations, the amount could be far greater. If you had a one-hundred-dollar bill in your pocket, it would be useless unless you directed it and used it efficiently. The bill cannot speak to you or give you any advice. Therefore, you need to activate it by using your mind, so the money becomes useful.

Depending on your thoughts and how you direct them, the money will follow in the same direction. If you use your mind wisely and direct the money to the right place, whether it is in savings, investing, real estate, corporate spending, and so forth, then that money will work in your favour. If, on the other hand, you use your mind irresponsibly, selfishly, carelessly, and so forth, then the money will not work in your favour; it will be more destructive than useful. Because we're on the subject of money, if you have had an opportunity and you think every given day your future holds no wealth or that you will remain as you are in your finances, then that is what your future will be. (Remember; your thoughts create energy and movement, they direct you)

Our perception and understanding of money can take us as far back as our childhood in the teachings and experiences given to us by our parents or caregivers. Since we depend on our parents to care for us financially, they instill beliefs and core values in relation to money and finances. For example, if you're brought up in a family that had low income, you would experience less spending, more rationing of money, more financial struggle and hardships, and so forth. Living in this environment, you may hear things like, "We can't afford that; we don't have the money to pay for it." You also witness and experience daily struggles that your parents or caregivers have gone through in order to move on. You may witness food rationing, clothing being passed down from siblings, fewer of the finer things in life, and so forth. So you build a sense of value and understanding towards money. This understanding may include the idea that making money isn't easy, and it's hard to come by; you only have so much, so you can only spend so much; I will never be rich, and so forth.

If, on the other hand, you were brought up with a family of high income, you experience more spending, less rationing with money, less financial struggles and hardships. You are able to enjoy the finer things in life. By living in this environment, you will hear things like, "We can afford it; we have the finances to buy it" or, "Why settle for less when you can have more?" Through this experience, you create a core understanding of money that may include ideas like money will make money, and it's easy to come by; spending money is no issue. I have the money; therefore, I can afford to buy it.

Through our entire life, we always reflect on the core values and understandings that have been instilled in us as children. We always look back on those experiences and never lose sight of them. As adults, we take responsibility for our finances.

Through our core values and understandings, we apply those principles to money. With this in mind, we also build our own perception and way of understanding money. From my experience as a child, I was told, "If you don't have the money, don't buy it until you do have the money." It was a very important lesson because it was a simple truth. How can you own something without paying for it first?

So it became common practice for me to save money before I bought something I wanted. The best understanding of this concept is that I owned it and had no debt! Let us not be mistaken, on certain items, you need to carry debt and build equity in order to pay for it. My concern today is our ways and habits of spending money and how we get connected to resources and financial institutions that will lend you money, whether you have good or bad credit. It is easier now than ever before to spend money we don't even have. It is so easy to simply get a line of credit or a credit card, go out and purchase items or services on it, and make a minimum monthly payment. I remember as a child seeing advertisements on the Visa card which, at that time, was called Charge Ex. It was one of the first credit cards issued. I can relate to a credit card called Charge Ex. It sounds more direct and to the point. The first part, Charge, which would imply a cost to purchase, and the last part, Ex, which would imply an expense, sounded like a fair name for what the card was meant to do in those days: charge an expense to you. (Later on, they changed the name to Visa). Since then, the marketing and concept of a credit card has changed greatly. Everyone today is on board with this concept of payment. From financial institutions, large retail stores, to smaller independent ones, everyone has tapped into this way of selling because it seems so convenient to the consumer.

Today, we have many products and means associated with this way of spending and attracting customers. There are incentives to motivate the consumer to spend and encourage them to use their card. Whether it be Aero Gold Card (so you're able to accumulate points or miles and receive a flight incentive of your destination), or a Sears card you can use with incentives to buy goods. If you like the option, you can even get a platinum card or a no-limit spending card. These cards are different in appearance and features; they come in a variety of colors, depending on your status and so on. There doesn't seem to be a shortage of cards for any needs.

The unfortunate drawback of using this type of card is high interest rates. The focus and marketing strategies glorifies the usage of these cards and emphasizes the rewards consumers receive by using the cards, rather focusing on the high interest rates that you're charged when not making full payment. One great example is when a major retailer has a sale and promotes, "no payment or interest for one year" (giving you all the time to make payment). It's a great incentive and it's convenient for the consumer, because the consumer does not have to pay on the day of purchase. *Caution*: If the consumer does not make full payment when it is due, the consumer is charged interest from the day they purchased the item, at rates of up to 25percent or higher. The retailer and financial institution has no problem with this; it's a great way for them to make additional money from you. You become the winner with this concept when you make full payment when payment is due. You lose out when you carry a balance. That balance, including interest, is compounded daily until it's fully paid. Until it's fully paid you are in *debt!* So enjoy all the incentives and promotions that you are entitled to at the time of purchase, or even the trip that you've always imagined on your Aero Miles Card that you've accumulated and, hopefully, at that time of your trip, the expenses that you incurred were paid up in full without any interest.

I feel, in all fairness, we should rename these cards and have more of a direct approach, as it was in the beginning with the credit card called Charge Ex. I would name these cards or this concept the "More Debt Card." After all, this is simply what we are applying for—more debt. Therefore, everything can be labelled as the More Debt Card. (Remember, you don't own it until you fully pay for it!) This can also apply when purchasing a home. Instead of using the *mortgage loan*, we can use the same concept and name it the "More Debt Loan." It all makes sense, because what we're doing is accruing more debt. It really gets you thinking when you eliminate misconceptions and distractions and are faced with the simple truth.

I would like to share with you another simple truth. I have been mentioning the fact that, if it isn't fully paid for, you don't own it. This is a partial truth. This overall truth is simply this: when it's paid in full, you own it for as long as you're living on this planet. After that, it isn't yours any more. So if you truly think about it, you're actually borrowing it until your time is up, then someone else comes along and takes over or makes use of it once it's fully paid for. So let us enjoy the things that are here and offered to us and take little ownership over them and not allow these things to control us, consume us, or define who we truly are. All things come and go. What we take and what remains with us is what we have stored in our *hearts!*

Thoughts and Expressions

You can gain more from someone who's achieved more than you.

To experience success in life, one must endure failure, for it is common to fail before you succeed.

It is more fulfilling to give, for if each one can give to another, everyone would be satisfied in receiving.

One who truly invests in one's heart will be rich.

With time comes opportunity.

For one to succeed one must endure failure.

When you love your occupation and you don't consider it to be work, you are truly living your purpose in life.

Passion for what you do is not considered work.

Materialistic love is only temporary but unfulfilling to the heart. Unconditional love is the greatest love of all.

NOTES FOR CHAPTER 5

Chapter Six
Understanding and Dealing with Three Major Obstacles in Life

Fear

Self esteem

Guilt

Fear

I believe there has been a time in our lives when each of us has experienced some form of fear. Newborn infants and children are receptive and extremely sensitive to their surroundings and, as you may have witnessed, it doesn't take much to startle or scare an infant or a child. We are exposed to fear at a young age, like if someone says, for example, "Don't go there or else the monster will get you." Parents and caregivers sometimes use fear as a way to control children. The child may experience fear in ways of physical, emotional, or verbal abuse. The child then carries the fears they've experienced into adult life. From childhood and into adult life, we allow the fear within us to limit our way of being, achieving, and doing in life. Fear destroys our dreams and desires. Earlier I described fear as an acronym: *False Evidence* that *Appears Real.* Fear is an emotion we know far too well so, therefore, it becomes one that has more control over us than we have over it. By having the fear within us, we set ourselves in a comfort zone and take little or no risk in the choices we make in our lives. As it has been used in our lives to control us, we automatically use fear to control others and our place in life.

Individuals who succeed financially usually take the risks involved in succeeding. They eliminate the fear, take the risks, and have the self-esteem and the determination to succeed. It's not unusual to hear a success story in which the individual who succeeded had to endure some sort of failure or set back at some point. We can link our fears with our past experiences. For example, if a child experiences the fear of being alone or being abandoned, that child will likely take the experience into his or her adult life. To avoid this fear, the adult will do what it takes to satisfy the fear within him. He or she my put the effort into finding the need to have someone close in their life so they won't feel alone or abandoned. Fear manifests from what we don't know and what we can't see, the unknown, or "what if." Fear also sets in when we feel powerless.

Let's look at some examples. When you are uncertain, you fear the outcome, so you hold back. You may think, "I'm uncertain about what may happen and I don't know what the outcome will be, so it's best that I don't take any chances. Who knows what might happen?" Feeling powerless over someone or a situation will also instill the fear in you. In truth, fear (false evidence that appears real) is all made up. If you apply truth and reason to your fears, you will see that they stem from the unknown or "what if." Fear in most cases is more of an illusion than it is real. Certain individuals will always feed on those who are fearful; they become easy prey. When you give into fear it will have control over you. One needs no courage if they have no fear.

Since I have experienced my epiphany I know and feel a connection with a higher power. I feel well protected from the power of any negativity and evil, for this higher power is at all times in full control. Being connected to this greater power and energy of goodwill, thoughts, and intentions to mankind is the greatest power of all. I reserve great respect to this higher power because this divine and infinite power will prevail, restore, and give life. Nothing will stand in its way; it will conquer all, including the power of evil and negativity.

Self-Esteem

Personal self-esteem, or lack of it, comes from your opinion of yourself and how worthy you think you are. How you feel about yourself has a direct effect on how you feel with others. As a child, I grew up with self-esteem issues. Being told by my parents at a young age that I wasn't worthy, capable or smart enough to achieve made me believe what I was told. When I entered grade one and failed, I believed it even more. So my belief was confirmed. I was first told by my parents (my first teachers) and in grade one, my school teacher (my second teacher) told me. This had a great impact on my self-esteem in the early stages of my life. It was more of a setback than anything else. It limited me from living life and achieving.

My grades in school were average or below average. I struggled every day just to get by. I never took chances or risks because I never believed in myself. For years, I focused on this distorted belief that had been passed on to me at a young age, when I was young, vulnerable and had no experience or understanding. I was just a kid and I did what young kids do: I listened, observed, and learned from my parents and others around me. It was only later in life, when I took responsibility to find truth and reason about my distorted belief that the truth surfaced. I discovered that I was able to achieve any goal I desired. I also accepted that the attempt in trying was just as important as achieving.

In all truth, you will never achieve if you don't try. I believe self-esteem issues originate from childhood and continue into teenage years. All you need to do is hear it more than once from a parent, a schoolteacher, a close family member, a friend, and so forth, and you will believe it. If someone does not speak highly of you, chances are they don't think highly of themselves. Low self-esteem will limit you in life and your achievements. High self-esteem will result in the opposite. Individuals who are highly successful and high achievers usually don't lack self-esteem or confidence. They believe in themselves and are not influenced by others and the negativity that surrounds them.

We all have the power to achieve whatever our hearts and mind desire. It's entirely up to us, no one else. Do not allow anyone to define who you are or pull you way from the truth that you're a wonderful, beautiful human being. You are worthy and capable. This is the simple truth; everything else is distorted and untrue.

Guilt

We can be our worst enemy. We take on a great amount of guilt for what we feel we have no power or control over. We also take blame for things that have happened in other people's lives, believing that it's entirely our fault. Guilt is also passed on from person to person. When someone isn't able to deal with his or her own issues, the first thing that person does is point the finger at someone else. Over time, the person being blamed starts to feel guilty and takes on the other person's role and his or her responsibility. I believe that if we can all build the courage and take the responsibility for ourselves and not blame others, the world would be a better place. It is important to take responsibility for our actions and our feelings. We must not take the responsibility of the issues, actions, and feelings of others. We as wonderful, beautiful human beings must take the responsibility of being compassionate, supportive, understanding, and loving. It isn't our responsibility to own the issues and the pain of others. It's entirely up to the individual to deal with the issues in which they're faced with.

In life, we go on a journey and come across many obstacles and unanswered questions. We simply don't have all the answers to what life unfolds before us. We feel guilty at times when we can't find the solution or answers to certain situations or occurrences that happen in our lives. Since we're not perfect, we make mistakes along the way and feel guilty, blaming ourselves and others. We must accept that it isn't our responsibility to have all the answers and solutions to life. If we had all the answers to life and the challenges it holds, life would be boring. Making mistakes in life gives us great opportunity to learn from them; it's a learning process. Without making mistakes, we simply cannot learn or know the difference. What concerns me is when someone makes the same mistakes over and over, expecting a different result in return.

At the start of every day, I make an affirmation that goes like this: "God has given me this day to do the best that I can with what I have and what I know, and that I will not create any resistance to what happens, for I will accept that I don't have control over everything, and what occurs is part of the plan." By making this affirmation, I accept and limit my stress, guilt, and control to find resolution to the results that appear. You need to stop feeling guilty and being so hard on yourself. You're only human, and you are entitled to make mistakes. When you make mistakes, you must think positively and use the opportunity to learn from them, so you don't repeat the same mistakes, spinning your wheels and going nowhere.

Thoughts and Expressions

You will not succeed if you do not proceed. Proceed with the purpose and the intent of taking positive action.

Takers will be taken, givers will be given.

Do not allow anyone to take away the power within you. You have the power to be, to do, and to have anything in life.

Infinite mind—the potential of the mind is limitless

The power of your mind can convince you of the things in life that are not true. Be careful of how you think. Take control over your mind and your thoughts, or your mind and thoughts will take control over you.

The most important person you need to get along with is you. You sleep with you and wake up with you every single day.

One needs no courage if one has no fear.

The most important moment in your life is now!

You are who you choose to do and be.

A healthy way of thinking will bring a healthy way of living.

NOTES FOR CHAPTER 6

Chapter Seven
Healthy Recipes for the Mind and Soul

Stress

- Accept the fact that you do not have control over everything.
- In having expectations, accept that there may be a different outcome for the circumstances that appear. Life revolves around all of us, not through you solely.
- Create no resistance to what appears or what happens, for it is the perfect plan.
- Stop wasting your time and energy trying to fix everything, serve everyone, and find all the answers. You don't need to.
- Do the best you can with what you know and what you have, and accept it.
- Go with the flow, not against it. It takes less effort.

- Don't take on other people's stress; it isn't your responsibility.
- You don't need to say yes to everything. You have the power and choice to say no.
- Don't be concerned with what other people think or their opinion of you. It isn't your responsibility to fulfill them.
- Worry and fear will stress you out! Eliminate them or they may eliminate you, for they are among the worst ingredients in life.
- Negative thoughts will take the energy right out of you and stress you out.
- Stress is a condition that we sometimes place on ourselves. Have control over stress or stress will have control over you and your life.

Relationships:

- In a close relationship, always play on the same team.
- Stop trying to win over your partner or be always right. You should always be on the same team.
- Respect each other's differences and opinions, for you are both two separate individuals.

- When conflict arises, always turn towards, not away from, each other.
- Take time out in the heat of the moment to regain your composure and your thoughts.
- Pay close attention and give thought to your words, for the words you speak have power.
- Listen to each other, not just to yourself.
- Be understanding, compassionate, forgiving, and loving towards each other.
- Love and respect yourself so you're able to share it with others.
- Relationships work best when everyone contributes in giving. It becomes fair for everyone so that, in receiving, everyone is satisfied. Use a give-and-take and take-and-give approach.

The Workplace

- Make your workplace a place you enjoy going to.
- Set personal goals to achieve more so you're motivated and driven. It gives you purpose to be there.
- Don't consider your workplace as just a job; if you do, you shouldn't be there.

- Have integrity and be authentic to your co-workers as well as yourself.
- Don't take issues personally in your workplace.
- Set aside time for personal issues away from the workplace; they don't mix with co-workers.
- View criticism in an optimistic way and always be positive.
- You get what you put into it. The greater your effort, the greater the result.
- The person who will best represent you in your workplace is you.
- Always reward yourself when you do well and achieve.
- Believe in yourself and never give up.
- If you have an off day, be more optimistic and hopeful for tomorrow.
- Always work as a team—*t*ogether *e*veryone *a*chieves *m*ore

True Success

- Life's success starts and ends with you.
- Your success in life depends on the attitude you choose.
- To define complete life success, one must include personal wealth, health, love, and

impeccable self-expression and representation of oneself.

- To experience success in life, you must endure failure, for it is common to fail before you succeed.
- Succeeding in life is doing something that you don't consider as *work*.
- Success is a matter of attitude.
- Life's success is in giving first, not receiving.
- To succeed in life one must form a partnership between the heart and mind.
- The greatest partners you will ever have in business are the heart and mind, which are conditioned to endure and succeed.
- True success covers four principals:
  1. Health
  2. Wealth
  3. Love
  4. Impeccable self representation and expression.

Achieving Goals and Fulfilling Your Dreams

- Everything starts with a thought or a dream—you just have to believe them.
- Trust and believe in yourself.

- Goals and dreams are possible. You must believe and take action.
- Time and patience is needed to achieve your goals and dreams.
- You must be able to endure failure in order to achieve your goals.
- Focus on positive thinking.
- Avoid being pessimistic by being more optimistic.
- Have a positive attitude towards your goals and dreams.
- Stay the course of personal empowerment and the empowerment of others to fulfill your goals and dreams.
- Avoid negative energy or anyone associated with negative thinking. This will only set you back.
- Don't procrastinate and take time for granted; time is of the essence. Without time there is no opportunity.

Self-Esteem

- Believe in yourself and allow no one else to take away the power within you or tell you otherwise.

- Don't let others dictate and tell you that it isn't possible. In truth it is possible if you believe in yourself.
- Don't believe you can't, because if you don't try you'll never know.
- Making mistakes is part of a learning process. Allow yourself the opportunity to learn from your mistakes.
- Forgive yourself for making mistakes. You're not perfect, and that's okay, because no one is perfect.
- Believe in the truth that you are a wonderful, beautiful human being and that you're able to do, to be, and to have anything in life. Allow no one to take away this power and understanding of who you truly are.
- Come to understand and realize when someone tells you how they feel about you and what they think of you, it is a direct representation, feeling, and expression of themselves.

Being at Peace

- Take the responsibility of knowing the truth of your past.

- Be compassionate towards yourself and others.
- Learn from your past, and then set it free.
- Forgive everyone, including yourself.
- Have no hate for anyone.
- Don't become stuck on your past in the present moment; it will only become your future.
- Love unconditionally and give without conditions.
- Practice the law of non-resistance—go with the flow.
- Eliminate being right and finding all the solutions. You don't have to.
- Accept everyone for their uniqueness, including yourself.
- Practice the act of love towards yourself and others every day.

Note:

Following these recipes for your mind and soul will make your life easier, more fulfilling, meaningful, and more loving and peaceful. Chances are you'll live longer and be more content and happier along the way in your life.

THIS IS NOT THE END.
IT IS THE BEGINNING.

Made in the USA
Charleston, SC
30 May 2010